The Earth's Surface

C O N C E P T   S C I E N C E

Written by Colin Walker • Illustrated by Sally Simons

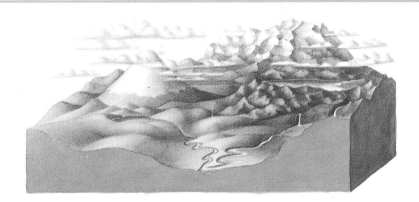

If we stand on a high hill,
we can see the shape of
the earth's surface.
We can see hills and mountains,
valleys and plains.

4

Big rivers and little streams
flow over the surface of the earth
into the sea.

There are deep canyons on the
surface of the earth.

There are lakes in deep hollows on the surface of the earth.

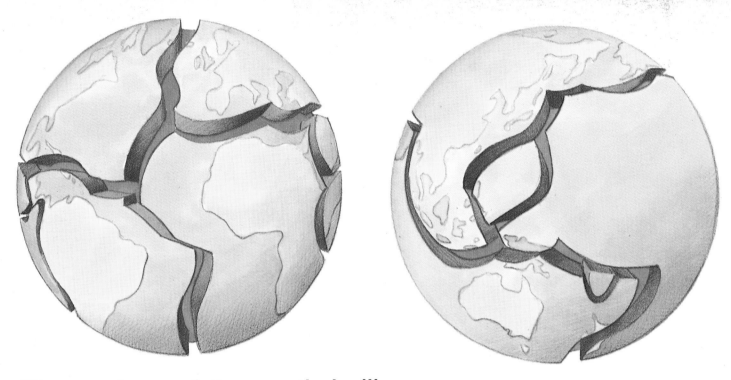

The surface of the earth is like a
giant jigsaw puzzle.
It is made up of big pieces called plates.
Forces in the earth
often push the plates against each other.

8

When the plates move,
we may feel an earthquake.

There are also plates under the sea.
There are even mountains,
canyons, and volcanoes under the sea!

Sometimes when a volcano erupts
under the sea, the sea water boils.
If there is a really big eruption,
a new island may be formed.

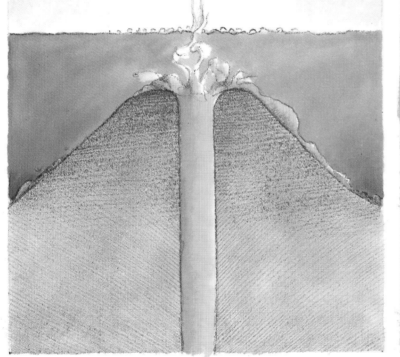
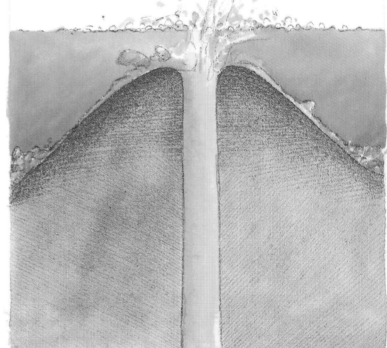

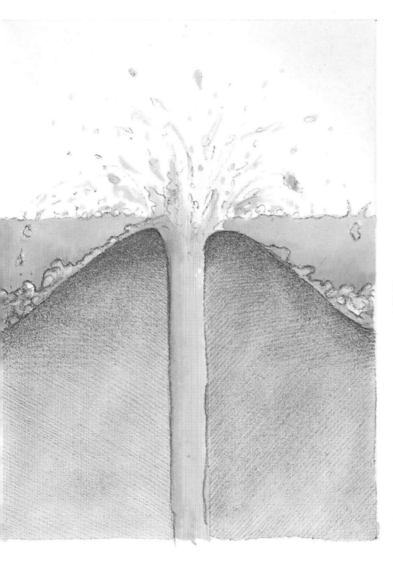

The earth's surface does not stay the same.
It has been changing for millions of years,
and it is still changing.

QUIZ

Ask your friend these questions. . .

Does the earth's surface stay the same?

Name these shapes formed
by the earth's surface.

What do we call the giant pieces
of the earth's surface?

Are there
under the sea?

How long has the earth's
surface been changing?